BARRY LOPEZ was born in 1945 in Port Chester, New York. He grew up in southern California, attended school in New York City and worked in Wyoming before graduating with honors from the University of Notre Dame. His books include OF WOLVES AND MEN, for which he received the John Burroughs Medal for distinguished Natural History writing; RIVER NOTES, a companion volume to DESERT NOTES; and GIVING BIRTH TO THUNDER, a collection of trickster stories. He is a contributing editor of *North American Review* and writes regularly for *Harper's* and other magazines. He lives with his wife in Oregon.

Avon Books are available at special quantity discounts for
bulk purchases for sales promotions, premiums, fund
raising or educational use. Special books, or book excerpts,
can also be created to fit specific needs.

For details write or telephone the office of the Director of
Special Markets, Avon Books, Dept. FP, 1790 Broadway,
New York, New York 10019, 212-262-3361.

DESERT NOTES
Reflections in the Eye of a Raven

BARRY HOLSTUN LOPEZ

 A BARD BOOK/PUBLISHED BY AVON BOOKS

"Desert Notes" originally appeared in slightly different form in *Skywriting;* "Coyote and Rattlesnake" originally appeared in *Northwest Review;* "Twilight" appeared in the *North American Review.*

Cover photograph by Barry Holstun Lopez
Design by Donald Johnson

AVON BOOKS
A division of
The Hearst Corporation
1790 Broadway
New York, New York 10019

First Bard Printing, February, 1981

The Sheed, Andrews & McMell, Inc. edition contains the
following Library of Congress Cataloging in Publication
Data:

Lopez, Barry Holstun, 1945-
Desert Notes.
1. Deserts—Addresses, essays, lectures. I. Title.

for Mary and Adrian

CONTENTS

In calling up images of the past, I find that the plains of Patagonia frequently cross before my eyes; yet these plains are pronounced by all wretched and useless.

They can be described only by negative characters; without habitations, without water, without trees, without mountains, they support merely a few dwarf plants. Why then, and the case is not peculiar to myself, have these arid wastes taken so firm a hold on my memory? Why have not the still more level, the greener and more fertile Pampas, which are serviceable to mankind, produced an equal impression?

I can scarcely analyze these feelings: but it must be partly owing to the free scope given to the imagination.

The plains of Patagonia are boundless, for they are scarcely passable, and hence unknown: they bear the stamp of having lasted, as they are now, for ages, and there seems no limit to their duration through future time. If, as the ancients supposed, the flat earth was surrounded by an impassable breadth of water, or by deserts heated to an intolerable excess, who would not look to these last boundaries to man's knowledge with deep but ill-defined sensations?

Charles Darwin, *The Voyage of the Beagle,* 1836

INTRODUCTION

With the Desert Fathers you have the characteristic
of a clean break with a conventional, accepted social
context in order to swim for one's life into an
apparently irrational void.

Thomas Merton

The land does not give easily. The desert is like a
boulder; you expect to wait. You expect night to come.
Morning. Winter to set in. But you expect sometime it
will loosen into pieces to be examined.

When it doesn't, you weary. You are no longer
afraid of its secrets, cowed by its silence. You break
away, angry, a little chagrined. You will tell anyone the
story: so much time spent for nothing. In the retelling
you sense another way inside; you return immediately
to the desert. The opening evaporates, like a vision
through a picket railing.

You can't get at it this way. You must come with
no intentions of discovery. You must overhear things,
as though you'd come into a small and desolate town
and paused by an open window. You can't learn
anything from saguaro cactus, from ocotillo. They are
just passing through; their roots, their much heralded
dormancy in the dry season, these are only illusions of
permanence. They know even less than you do.

You have to proceed almost by accident. I learned
about a motor vehicle this way.

I was crossing the desert. Smooth. Wind rippling at
the window. There was no road, only the alkaline

plain. There was no reason for me to be steering; I let go of the wheel. There was no reason to sit where I was; I moved to the opposite seat. I stared at the empty driver's seat. I could see the sheen where I'd sat for years. We continued to move across the desert.

I moved to the back of the vehicle — a large van with windows all around — and sat by the rear doors. I could hear the crushing of earth beneath the wheels. I opened the doors wide and leaned out. I saw the white alkaline surface of the desert slowly emerging from under the sill, as though the van were fixed in space and the earth turning beneath us.

I opened all the doors. The wind blew through.

I stepped out; ran away. When I stopped and turned around the vehicle was moving east. I ran back to it and jumped in. Out the driver's door; in through the back. I got out again, this time with my bicycle, and rode north furiously until the vehicle was only a speck moving on the horizon behind me. I curved back and crossed slowly in front of it. I could hear the earth crumbling under the crush of my rubber tires and the clicketing of my derailleur gears. I lay the bike down and jogged alongside the vehicle, the padding of my sneakers next to the hiss of the rolling tire. I shifted it into neutral through the open door and turned the key off. I sat in it until it came to rest. I walked back for the bicycle.

Until then I did not understand how easily the vehicle's tendencies of direction and movement could be abandoned, together with its systems of roads, road signs, and stop lights. By a series of strippings such as this one enters the desert.

When I first came into the desert I was arrested by the space first, especially what hung in a layer just above the dust of the desert floor. The longer I regarded it the clearer it became that its proportion had limits, that it had an identity, like the air around a stone. I suspected that everything I'd come here to find out was hidden inside that sheet of space.

I developed methods of inquiry, although I appeared to be doing nothing at all. I appeared completely detached. I appeared to be smelling my hands cupped full of rocks. I appeared to be asleep. But I was not. Even inspecting an abandoned building at some distance from the desert I would glance over in that direction, alert. I was almost successful. Toward the end of my inquiry I moved with exquisite ease. But I could not disguise the waiting.

One morning as I stood watching the sun rise, washing out the blue black, watching the white crystalline stars fade, my bare legs quivering in the cool air, I noticed my hands had begun to crack and turn to dust.

DESERT NOTES

I know you are tired. I am tired too. Will you walk along the edge of the desert with me? I would like to show you what lies before us.

All my life I have wanted to trick blood from a rock. I have dreamed about raising the devil and cutting him in half. I have thought too about never being afraid of anything at all. This is where you come to do those things.

I know what they tell you about the desert but you mustn't believe them. This is no deathbed. Dig down, the earth is moist. Boulders have turned to dust here, the dust feels like graphite. You can hear a man breathe at a distance of twenty yards. You can see out there to the edge where the desert stops and the mountains begin. You think it is perhaps ten miles. It is more than a hundred. Just before the sun sets all the colors will change. Green will turn to blue, red to gold.

I've been told there is very little time left, that we must get all these things about time and place straight. If we don't, we will only have passed on and have changed nothing. That is why we are here I think, to change things. It is why I came to the desert.

Here things are sharp, elemental. There's no one to look over your shoulder to find out what you're doing with your hands, or to ask if you have considered the number of people dying daily of malnutrition. If you've been listening you must suspect that a knife will be very useful out here — not to use, just to look at.

There is something else here, too, even more important: explanations will occur to you, seeming to clarify; but they can be a kind of trick. You will think you have hold of the idea when you only have hold of its clothing.

Feel how still it is. You can become impatient here, willing to accept any explanation in order to move on. This appears to be nothing at all, but it is a wall between you and what you are after. Be sure you are not tricked into thinking there is nothing to fear. Moving on is not important. You must wait. You must take things down to the core. You must be careful with everything, even with what I tell you.

This is how to do it. Wait for everything to get undressed and go to sleep. Forget to explain to yourself why you are here. Listen attentively. Just before dawn you will finally hear faint music. This is the sound of the loudest dreaming, the dreams of boulders. Continue to listen until the music isn't there. What you thought about boulders will evaporate and what you know will become clear. Each night it will be harder. Listen until you can hear the dreams of the dust that settles on your head.

I must tell you something else. I have waited out here for rattlesnakes. They never come. The moment eludes me and I hate it. But it keeps me out here. I would like to trick the rattlesnake into killing itself. I would like this kind of finality. I would like to begin again with the snake. If such a thing were possible, the desert would be safe. You could stay here forever.

I will give you a few things: bits of rock, a few twigs, this shell of a beetle blown out here by the wind. You should try to put the bits of rock back together to form a stone, although I cannot say that all these pieces are from the same stone. If they don't fit together look for others that do. You should try to coax some leaves from these twigs. You will first have to determine whether they are alive or dead. And you will have to find out what happened to the rest of the beetle, the innards. When you have done these things you will know a little more than you did before. But be careful. It will occur to you that these tasks are silly or easily done. This is a sign, the first one, that you are being fooled.

I hope you won't be here long. After you have finished with the stone, the twigs and the beetle, other things will suggest themselves, and you must take care of them. I see you are already tired. But you must stay. This is the pain of it all. You can't keep leaving.

Do you hear how silent it is? This will be a comfort as you work. Do not laugh. When I first came here I laughed very loud and the sun struck me across the face and it took me a week to recover. You will only lose time by laughing.

I will leave you alone to look out on the desert. What makes you want to leave now is what is trying to kill you. Have the patience to wait until the rattlesnake kills itself. Others may tell you that this has already happened, and this may be true. But wait until you see for yourself, until you are sure.

THE
HOT
SPRING

I.

The man would set off late in the spring, after the dogwood had bloomed, in the blue '58 Chevy pickup with the broken taillight and the cracked Expando mirrors. He would take a thin green sleeping bag and a blue tarpaulin, a few dishes and a one-burner stove. He would take his spoon and only cereal to eat and tea to drink. He would take no books, no piece of paper to write on.

He would stop only for gas and would pick up no hitchhikers. He would drive straight through on the two-lane, blacktop roads, cracked and broken with the freeze of last winter, without turning the radio on. He would lift his damp buttocks from the hot naugahyde seat and let the wind, coming in through the window that was stuck halfway down, cool him.

It would take seven hours to drive the 278 miles. First, over the mountains, past the great lava flows at the ridge, past the slopes of black obsidian glass, down into the sweet swamp of thick air in the ponderosa forest.

He would drive out then into the great basin over arroyos and across sage flats dotted with juniper and rabbit brush, past the fenced squares marked Experimental Station where the government was trying to grow crested wheat grass, trying to turn the high desert into grassy fields for bony Herefords with vacant

9

eyes. He would see few cows. He would see, on a long stretch of road, a golden eagle sitting on a fence post.

There would be more space between the towns and more until there were no towns at all, only empty shacks, their roof ridges bowed, their doors and windows gone.

He would come around the base of another range of mountains, slip down on the southeastern side and drive on a one-lane dirt road along the edge of the alkaline desert for twenty miles until he came to the hot spring. There he would stop. He would stop the truck, but he would leave the motor running to keep the engine cool. He would always arrive by one in the afternoon.

II.

He inhaled the tart, sulphurous fumes rising up from the green reeds, the only bit of green for miles. He watched the spiders spinning webs in the wire grass and the water bugs riding the clots of yellow bubbles. He stared at the bullet-riddled walls of tin that surrounded the sandy basin where the water collected.

When he had seen these things, that they had weathered the winter, the man put the truck in gear and rolled down over the sagebrush and onto the desert floor. He drove out over the dry, bleached soil for a mile before he put the truck in neutral and let it coast to a stop. He was careful with the silence. He could hear his fingers slide over the plastic steering wheel. He could feel the curve of his lips tightening in the dryness.

He took off his clothes, all of them, and put them in a zippered airlines bag on the floor of the truck. Then he put his sneakers back on and went naked across the desert back to the hot spring with a pair of linen socks in his hand. The cool breeze from the mountains raised his flesh into a lattice of pin-pricked hills.

He removed his shoes. He lay on his back in the hot water, his toes grazing the shallow, sandy bottom of the pool. He could hear the water lapping at the entrance to his ears, the weight of water pulling on his hair; he could feel the particles of dust falling off his flesh, floating down, settling on the bottom of the pool; he could feel the water prying at the layers of dried sweat. He concentrated and tried to hear the dirt and sweat breaking away from his body. The tips of his fingers wrinkled, and he stared at the water pooling in the cavity of his chest and falling away as he breathed.

He wanted to stay until the sun set but he couldn't: he could feel himself sinking. He climbed out of the pool and walked out of the roofless tin shelter onto the floor of the desert. The wind began to evaporate the water and his pores closed like frightened mussels and trapped the warmth beneath his skin.

When his feet were dry he put on only the linen socks and left. He could feel the wind eddying up around him like a cloak and his feet barely touched the ground. His eyes felt smoother in their sockets and he could tell, without looking, how his fingers were curled; he could see the muscles of his legs tied beneath his kneecaps, feel the patella gliding over the knot. He felt the muscles anchored on the broad, flat plate of his hipbones and the wind soft deep in the roots of his

11

hair. He felt the pressure of his parting the air as he walked.

When he got back to the truck he poured a cup of water and placed a handful of cereal into an earthen bowl. He ate and looked out across the desert and imagined that he had come to life again.

THE
RAVEN

I am going to have to start at the other end by telling you this: there are no crows in the desert. What appear to be crows are ravens. You must examine the crow, however, before you can understand the raven. To forget the crow completely, as some have tried to do, would be like trying to understand the one who stayed without talking to the one who left. It is important to make note of who has left the desert.

To begin with, the crow does nothing alone. He cannot abide silence and he is prone to stealing things, twigs and bits of straw, from the nests of his neighbors. It is a game with him. He enjoys tricks. If he cannot make up his mind the crow will take two or three wives, but this is not a game. The crow is very accommodating and he admires compulsiveness.

Crows will live in street trees in the residential areas of great cities. They will walk at night on the roofs of parked cars and peck at the grit; they will scrape the pinpoints of their talons across the steel and, with their necks outthrust, watch for frightened children listening in their beds.

Put all this to the raven: he will open his mouth as if to say something. Then he will look the other way and say nothing. Later, when you have forgotten, he will tell you he admires the crow.

The raven is larger than the crow and has a beard of black feathers at his throat. He is careful to kill only what he needs. Crows, on the other hand, will search out the great horned owl, kick and punch him awake, and then, for roosting too close to their nests, they will kill him. They will come out of the sky on a fat, hot afternoon and slam into the head of a dozing rabbit and go away laughing. They will tear out a whole row of planted corn and eat only a few kernels. They will defecate on scarecrows and go home and sleep with 200,000 of their friends in an atmosphere of congratulation. Again, it is only a game; this should not be taken to mean that they are evil.

There is however this: when too many crows come together on a roost there is a lot of shoving and noise and a white film begins to descend over the crows' eyes and they go blind. They fall from their perches and lie on the ground and starve to death. When confronted with this information, crows will look past you and warn you vacantly that it is easy to be misled.

The crow flies like a pigeon. The raven flies like a hawk. He is seen only at a great distance and then not very clearly. This is true of the crow too, but if you are very clever you can trap the crow. The only way to be sure what you have seen is a raven is to follow him until he dies of old age, and then examine the body.

Once there were many crows in the desert. I am told it was like this: you could sit back in the rocks and watch a pack of crows working over the carcass of a coyote. Some would eat, the others would try to squeeze out the vultures. The raven would never be seen. He would be at a distance, alone, perhaps eating a scorpion.

There was, at this time, a small alkaline water hole at the desert's edge. Its waters were bitter. No one but crows would drink there, although they drank sparingly, just one or two sips at a time. One day a raven warned someone about the dangers of drinking the bitter water and was overheard by a crow. When word of this passed among the crows they felt insulted. They jeered and raised insulting gestures to the ravens. They bullied each other into drinking the alkaline water until they had drunk the hole dry and gone blind.

The crows flew into canyon walls and dove straight into the ground at forty miles an hour and broke their necks. The worst of it was their cartwheeling across the desert floor, stiff wings outstretched, beaks agape, white eyes ballooning, surprising rattlesnakes hidden under sage bushes out of the noonday sun. The snakes awoke, struck and held. The wheeling birds strew them across the desert like sprung traps.

When all the crows were finally dead, the desert bacteria and fungi bored into them, burrowed through bone and muscle, through aqueous humor and feathers until they had reduced the stiff limbs of soft black to blue dust.

After that, there were no more crows in the desert. The few who watched from a distance took it as a sign and moved away.

Finally there is this: one morning four ravens sat at the edge of the desert waiting for the sun to rise. They had been there all night and the dew was like beads of quicksilver on their wings. Their eyes were closed and they were as still as the cracks in the desert floor.

The wind came off the snow-capped peaks to the north and ruffled their breath feathers. Their talons arched in the white earth and they smoothed their wings with sleek, dark bills. At first light their bodies swelled and their eyes flashed purple. When the dew dried on their wings they lifted off from the desert floor and flew away in four directions. Crows would never have had the patience for this.

If you want to know more about the raven: bury yourself in the desert so that you have a commanding view of the high basalt cliffs where he lives. Let only your eyes protrude. Do not blink — the movement will alert the raven to your continued presence. Wait until a generation of ravens has passed away. Of the new generation there will be at least one bird who will find you. He will see your eyes staring up out of the desert floor. The raven is cautious, but he is thorough. He will sense your peaceful intentions. Let him have the first word. Be careful: he will tell you he knows nothing.

If you do not have the time for this, scour the weathered desert shacks for some sign of the raven's body. Look under old mattresses and beneath loose floorboards. Look behind the walls. Sooner or later you will find a severed foot. It will be his and it will be well preserved.

Take it out in the sunlight and examine it closely. Notice that there are three fingers that face forward, and a fourth, the longest and like a thumb, that faces to the rear. The instrument will be black but no longer shiny, the back of it sheathed in armor plate and the underside padded like a wolf's foot.

At the end of each digit you will find a black, curved talon. You will see that the talons are not as sharp as you might have suspected. They are made to grasp and hold fast, not to puncture. They are more like the jaws of a trap than a fistful of ice picks. The subtle difference serves the raven well in the desert. He can weather a storm on a barren juniper limb; he can pick up and examine the crow's eye without breaking it.

18

TWILIGHT

I am sitting on a storm pattern rug woven out of the mind of a Navajo woman, Ahlnsaha, and traded to a man named Dobrey in Winslow, Arizona, for groceries in August 1934.

In the fall of 1936 a Swedish farmer, Kester Vorland, his land gone out from under him in the Depression, leaves his wife and three children in the car and, picking his moment perfectly, steps back into the store to steal the rug while Dobrey is busy in the back with a broken saddle. He trades it the next day in Flagstaff for groceries and $25 cash and moves on to Needles. It is bought later by a young man named Diego Martin who takes it back to San Bernardino, California, with him. He boasts of it to his friends, a piece of shrewd buying. When he is married in 1941 he gives it to his wife and, one flat September night, they make love on it, leaving a small stain that the girl, Yonella, can easily point out but which Diego will not believe, even when she shows him. He believes it is a stain left by an insect; he forbids her to show the rug to anyone after this. He dies in a bar fight in Honolulu on April 16, 1943, a corporal in the Marines. Yonella sells everything. An old woman with red hair and liver spots on her throat pouch named Elizabeth Reiner buys the rug for $45 and takes it home with her to Santa Barbara. In 1951 her daughter comes to visit and her grandson John Charles who is ten begins to covet the rug; when the mother and daughter fall into an

21

argument over something, the older woman angrily gives it to the boy (she snatches it down off the wall) as demonstration of her generosity. She later tells her daughter not to come back again and begins to miss the rug and feel foolish. The boy doesn't care. He vows he will always write her at Christmastime, even if his mother forbids it.

On the train from Los Angeles to Prairie du Chien the boy keeps himself wrapped in the rug like a turtle. He sits on the bed in his underwear with it over his shoulders and watches Nebraska. When he is sixteen John Charles falls in love with Dolores Patherway who is nineteen and a whore. One night she trades him twenty-five minutes for the blanket, but he does not see it this way: it is a gift, the best he can offer, a thing of power. That night she is able to sell it to a Great Lakes sailor for $60. She tells him it is genuine Sioux, there at the battle of the Little Big Horn, and will always bring a good price. The sailor's name is Benedict Langer, from a good Catholic family in Ramapo, New Jersey, and he has never had hard liquor or even VD but in three weeks in the service his father said would make a man of him he has lain in confusion with six different women who have told him he was terrific; he has sensed a pit opening. The day after he buys it Benedict gives the blanket to a friend, Frank Winter, and goes to look for a priest in Green Bay, the football town. In March 1959 Frank mails it to his parents for an anniversary present (it has been in his footlocker for eighteen months and smells like mothballs, a condition he remedies by airing it at night from the signal deck of the *U.S.S. Kissell*). He includes with it a document he has had made up in the ship's

22

print shop to the effect that it is an authentic Pawnee blanket, so his parents will be proud, can put it up on the wall of their retirement home in Boca Raton, Florida, next to the maracas from Guadalajara. They leave it in the box in the hall closet; they do not talk about it. Mr. Winter confides to his wife in the dark one night that he doesn't believe in the powers of medicine men.

On July 17, 1963, Frank Winter dies instantly when his foot hits a land mine in the Mekong Delta. His father waits a month before donating the blanket and the boy's other belongings to Catholic Charities. Father Peter Donnell, a local priest, a man of some sensitivity, lays the rug down on brown wall-to-wall carpeting in the foyer of the refectory of the Catholic Church in Boca Raton, arranging two chairs and a small table precisely on it (he likes especially the Ganado red color) before the Monsignor asks him to remove it. Father Donnell keeps the rug in his room, spread out flat under his mattress for a year. He takes it with him when he is transferred to Ames, Iowa, where it is finally bought in an Easter bazaar as Father Donnell endures a self-inflicted purging of personal possessions. It is bought by antique dealers, Mr. and Mrs. Theodore Wishton Spanner of Jordan Valley, Oregon (as they sign the register). The following winter I buy it from Mrs. Spanner who tells me the rug has been woven by a Comanche who learned his craft from a Navajo, that she bought it on the reservation in Oklahoma. It is certified. I take the rug home and at dusk I undress and lie down under it so that it completely covers my body. I listen all night. I do not hear anything. But in this time I am able to sort out all the smells buried in the threads and the sounds still reverberating deep in the fibers. It is what I have been looking for.

It is this rug I have carefully spread out now, east and west over the dust. It is only from such a height above the floor of the desert that one is able to see clearly what is going on.

The moon has just risen; the sun has just gone down. There are only a few stars up and a breeze is blowing up from the south. It smells like wet cottonwood leaves.

This is the best time to see what is happening. Everyone who is passing through will be visible for a short time. Already I have seen the priest with his Bible bound in wolves' fur and the blackbirds asleep in his hair.

I see the woman who smells like sagebrush and her three children with the large white eyes and tattered leggings. I see the boy who rolls in dust like a horse and the legionnaire with the alabaster skin polished smooth by the wind. I see the magnificent jethery loping across the desert like a greyhound with his arms full of oars. I watch cheetahs in silver chariots pulled by a span of white crows. I see the rainbow in arabesques of the wind.

The night gets deeper. I pull down to listen for Ahlnsaha: she is crying in Arizona. This is what she is singing:

> Go to the white rain
> Ta ta ta ta
> Go to the white rain

Ta ta ta ta
I see the horses
Ta ta ta ta
They are feeding above there.

There is no rain; there are no horses. Her music falls into pieces with her tears in the dust like lies. She smells like your face in wheat.

The moon is up higher, clearing the thin clouds on the horizon.

The two girls with the sun in a spiderweb bag are standing by the mountains south talking with the blue snake that makes holes in the wind with his whistle.

I can smell the heat of the day stuck on the edges of the cracks in the earth like a salt crust after a tide. I lay back and watch the sky. I close my eyes. I run my hands out smooth over the rug and feel the cold rising from the earth. When I come again I will bring a friar's robe with a deep cowl and shoes of jute fiber. I will run like a madman to the west all night until I begin to fall asleep; then I will walk back, being careful to correct for the tilt of the earth, the force of Coriolis, reading my breviary by the precise arrowlight of stars, assured of my destination.

The day hugs the desert floor like a fallen warrior. I am warm. I am alert for any sort of light. I believe there is someplace out there where you can see right down into the heart of the earth. The light there is strong enough to burn out your eyes like sap in a fire. But I won't go near it. I let it pass. I like to know that if I need it, with only a shovel or a small spade, I can begin digging and recall the day.

This time is the only time you will see the turtles massed on the eastern border for the march to the western edge where there is water, and then back the same night to hide in the bushes and smash insects dazed to lethargy in the cold. I have spoken with these turtles. They are reticent about their commitments. Each one looks like half the earth.

This is the only time you can study both of your shadows. If you sit perfectly still and watch your primary shadow as the sun sets you will be able to hold it long enough to see your other shadow fill up when the moon rises like a porcelain basin with clear water. If you turn carefully to face the south you may regard both of them: to understand the nature of silence you must be able to see into this space between your shadows.

This is the only time you will be able to smell water and not mistake it for the smell of a sheet of granite, or confuse it with the smell of marble or darkness. If you are moving about at this time, able to go anywhere you choose, you will find water as easily as if you were looking for your hands. It may take you some hours, even days to arrive at the place, but there will be no mistake about the direction to go once you smell it. The smell of water is not affected by the air currents so you won't need to know the direction of the wind; the smell of water lays along the surface of the earth like a long stick of peeled elmwood.

This is the only time you can hear the flight of the grey eagle over the desert. You cannot see him because he fades with the sun and is born out of it in the morning but it is possible to hear his wings pumping against the columns of warm air rising and hear the slip of the wind in his feathers as he tilts his gyre out over the desert floor. There is nothing out there for him, no rabbits to hunt, no cliff faces to fall from, no rock on which to roost, but he is always out there at this time fading to grey and then to nothing, turning on the wind with his eyes closed. It doesn't matter how high he goes or how far away he drifts, you will be able to hear him. It is only necessary to lie out flat somewhere and listen for the sound, like the wrinkling of the ocean.

The last thing you will notice will be the stones, small bits of volcanic ash, black glass, blue tourmaline, sapphires, narrow slabs of grey feldspar, rose quartz, sheets of mica and blood agate. They are small enough to be missed, laying down in the cracks of the desert floor, but they are the last things to give up the light; you will see them flare and burn like coals before they let go.

It is good to have a few of these kinds of stones with you in a pocket or cupped in your hand before you go to sleep. One man I knew, only for a short time, was sure the stones were more important than anything else; he kept a blue one tied behind his ear. One evening while we were talking he reached over and with a wet finger took alkaline dust and painted a small lightning bolt on his right cheek. I regarded him for more than an hour before it became too dark to see. I rolled myself up in this blanket and slept.

PERIMETER

I.

In the west, in the blue mountains, there are creeks of grey water. They angle out of the canyons, come across the brown scratched earth to the edge of the desert and run into nothing. When these creeks are running they make a terrific noise.

No one to my knowledge has ever counted the number, but I think there are more than twenty; it is difficult to be precise. For example, some of the creeks have been given names that, over the years, have had to be given up because a creek has run three or four times and then the channel has been abandoned.

You can easily find the old beds, where the dust has been washed out to reveal a level of rock rubble — cinnabar laced with mercury, fool's gold, clear quartz powder, and fire opal; but it is another thing to find one of the creeks, even when they are full. I have had some success by going at night and listening for the noise.

There is some vegetation in this area; it does not seem to depend on water. The rattlesnakes live here along with the rabbits. When there is any thunder it is coming from this direction. During the day the wind is here. The smells include the hellebore, vallo weed and punchen; each plant puts out its own smell and together they make a sort of pillow that floats a few feet off the ground where they are not as likely to be torn up by the wind.

II.

To the north the blue mountains go white and the creeks become more dependable though there are fewer of them. There is a sort of swamp here at the edge of the desert where the creeks pool and where grasses and sedges grow and the water takes a considerable time to evaporate and seep into the earth. There are some ducks here, but I do not know where they come from or where they go when the swamp dries up in the summer. I have never seen them flying. They are always hiding, slipping away; you will see their tail feathers disappearing in the screens of wire grass. They never quack.

There are four cottonwood trees here and two black locusts. The cottonwoods smell of balsam, send out seeds airborne in a mesh of exceedingly fine white hair, and produce a glue which the bees use to cement their honeycombs. Only one of the cottonwoods, the oldest one, is a female. The leaf stem meets the leaf at right angles and this allows the leaves to twitter and flash in the slightest breeze. The underside of the leaf is a silver green. I enjoy watching this windflash of leaves in strong moonlight.

The black locusts are smaller, younger trees and grow off by themselves a little. They were planted by immigrants and bear sweet smelling pea-like flowers with short, rose-like thorns at the leaf nodes. There are a few chokecherry bushes and also a juniper tree. You can get out of the sun here at noon and sleep. The wind runs down the sides of the cottonwoods like water and cools you.

An old tawny long-haired dog lives here.

Sometimes you will see him, walking along and always leaning to one side. There is also part of a cabin made with finished lumber lying on its back; the dark brown boards are dotted with red and yellow lichen and dry as sun-baked, long forgotten shoes.

III.

To the east the white mountains drop off and there is a flat place on the horizon and then the red mountains start. There is almost nothing growing in these mountains, just a little sagebrush. At the base, where they come to the desert, there are dunes, white like gypsum.

Inside the mountains are old creeks that run in circles over the floors of low-ceilinged caves. The fish in these waters are white and translucent; you can see a pink haze of organs beneath the skin. Where there should be eyes there are grey bulges that do not move. On the walls are white spiders like tight buttons of surgical cotton suspended on long hairy legs. There are white beetles, too, scurrying through the hills of black bat dung.

I have always been suspicious of these caves because the walls crumble easily under your fingertips; there is no moisture in the air and it smells like balloons. The water smells like oranges but has no taste. Nothing you do here makes any sound.

You have to squeeze through these red mountains to get around them; you can't walk over them. You have to wedge yourself in somewhere at the base and go in. There is always a moment of panic before you slip in when you are stuck. Your eyes are pinched shut and the heels of your shoes wedge and make you feel foolish.

At night the wind lies in a trough at the base of the red mountains, sprawled asleep over the white sand dunes like a caterpillar. The edge of the desert is most indistinct in this place where the white sand and the alkaline dust blow back and forth in eddies of the wind's breath while it sleeps.

IV.

In the south the red mountains fall away and yellow mountains rise up, full of silver and turquoise rock. There are plenty of rabbits here, a little rain in the middle of the summer, fine clouds tethered on the highest peaks. If you are out in the middle of the desert, this is the way you always end up facing.

In the south twelve buckskin horses are living along the edge of the yellow mountains. The creeks here are weak; the horses have to go off somewhere for water but they always come back. There is a little grass but the horses do not seem to eat it. They seem to be waiting, or finished. Ten miles away you can hear the clack of their hooves against the rocks. In the afternoon they are motionless, with their heads staring down at the ground, at the little stones.

At night they go into the canyons to sleep standing up.

From the middle of the desert even on a dark night you can look out at the mountains and perceive the differences in direction. From the middle of the desert you can see everything well, even in the black dark of a new moon. You know where everything is coming from.

THE
BLUE MOUND
PEOPLE

Once there was a people here who numbered, at their greatest concentration, perhaps two hundred. It has been determined by a close examination of their bones and careful reconstruction of muscle tissues that although they looked as we do they lacked vocal cords. They lived in caves ranged in tiers in the bluffs to the east on the far edge of the desert and because of this some of their more fragile belongings, even clothing, can still be examined intact. The scraps of cloth that have been found are most frequently linen, some of them woven of over a thousand threads to the inch, cloth the thickness of human hair. As nearly as can be determined, there were no distinctions in clothing between the sexes; everyone apparently wore similar linen robes of varying coarseness and sandals made of woven sage.

Also found in the caves were the usual implements: mortars and pestles, cooking knives, even some wooden bowls that, like the cloth, are oddly preserved. The knives are curious, made of silver and inlaid with black obsidian glass along the cutting edge. A number of glass and crystal shards have been found in the dirt on the floors of the caves, along with bits of bone china and porcelain. Some intact pieces have been uncovered and the workmanship is excellent. A pair of heavily worked pewter candlesticks together with scraps of beeswax were also located.

The caves, though with separate entrances, are linked by an odd and, it seems, needlessly complicated maze of interconnecting hallways. Nothing has been found in these hallways except where they juncture with caves; here a storage area seems to have existed, a sort of back porch. It has been theorized that the maze itself might have been a defensive network of some sort.

Other than the sharp implements apparently used in the preparation of food, there are no other weapons of any sort to be found. This at first puzzled archeologists, who had determined by an examination of shallow refuse pits that the cave people lived on a mixed and varied diet of meat and vegetables. Not only were no hunting implements found (not even ropes or materials for building snares), there were, it has been determined, too few animals nearby to account for the abundance revealed in an examination of the refuse pits and larder areas. Further complicating the issue of sustenance is the lack of evidence that soil suitable for farming was available to provide the many cultivated varieties of melon, tomato, cucumber, celery and other vegetables for which we have found fossilized seeds. Nor could there have been enough water without some form of irrigation (and there was no river at that time for that) to support such agriculture. In fact, a series of drillings has revealed that only enough water was available to support perhaps sixty to eighty people over the course of a year without exhausting the water table.

Radiocarbon dating has pinpointed the time of inhabitance at $22,000 \pm 1430$ years BP. Again, a projection of game populations and climatic conditions for this period indicates that the cave people were living a life of apparent plenty in an area that, clearly, could not support such an existence. It has been suggested that these people hunted and farmed abroad but preferred to live at the edge of the desert and traversed great distances in order to do so, but this suggestion has not been taken seriously. The nearest area with sufficient water and soil suitable for farming lies sixty miles to the northeast. Also there is this: the major source of meat, after rabbits and, strangely, geese, was a diminutive antelope, an extremely wary creature so widely scattered that it could not be effectively hunted by men on foot. Only very occasionally could such animals be tricked into running off a cliff or trapped in a piskun. It has been conjectured that they traded for their food but this is highly unlikely.

The question of how they provided for themselves remains unanswered.

Other questions also remain. For instance, no cause of death has been determined for the 173 sets of remains, but it is believed that they all died within the period of a year. All but one was arranged in a crypt in the walls of the caves. The one who was not was found sitting on the floor with his back against an intricately woven cedar bark backrest. This man was in his forties and was apparently working on a piece of beaded cloth when he died. It has never been suggested where his white alabaster beads came from.

What these people did is also a mystery; just as there are no hunting implements, so there are no agricultural tools. Nor is there evidence of elaborate religious ceremonies nor extensive artwork nor are there tools or ovens to work the glass and metal objects found in the caves (and it is extremely unlikely that these were obtained in trade as we know of no other cultural group with such skills in existence at this time).

Some believe that a key to understanding these people lies in determining the purpose of a series of blue earth mounds. These mounds of deep blue-grey dust are about a foot high and are perfectly conical in shape but for the rounded tops. One was found in each cave and the remains of four of them have been detected out on the desert, approximately a mile from the caves. At the heart of each one, toward the base, a hard white stone was found, perfectly round, smoother than dry marble, as if it had been washed for hundreds of years in a creek bed. These stones are gypsum-like but of a different crystalline structure and extremely light. There is some reason to believe that they are the fossilized remains of some sort of organism.

It is for this reason, of course, that these people are referred to as the People of the Blue Earth or the Blue Mound People. They cannot be associated, either geographically or by the level of certain of their crafts with any of their supposed contemporaries. And a number of questions continue to pose themselves. In spite of their anatomical inability to speak, we find no evidence of any other system of communication. No paintings, no writing, no systems of marking, no sequences of any sort. And there is, of course, no source for the linen cloth. There are no objects which might be called toys or evidence of any games, although several lute-like instruments have been found. Almost everything else is quite common in design but the materials from which some things have been made are unusual. There are, as I have indicated, pieces of china and glass, even sterling silver, but, as I have noted, no evidence of their fabrication. A careful sifting of cave soils has revealed fragments of oak and leather furniture but no evidence of fire pits, as, indeed there was at that time apparently no wood or other fuel close by. As nearly as can be determined, food was prepared on rock slabs outside the caves with perhaps some glass device to concentrate the rays of the sun. Inside the caves there was, it seems, no source of heat.

A single scrap of papyrus-like paper has been found and objects for which no explanation has been set forth (among them a smooth red sandstone disc and an enormous turtle shell) have also been appearing.

Further analysis of the cave soils and a closer examination of the surrounding area continues, but you can see the problem. We are dealing here with a people entirely out of the order of things and, for this reason, we should be forgiven any sort of speculation. An artist with an eastern museum, for example, has completed a series of drawings based on anatomical studies; he has given these people blue-grey skin and white hair with soft grey eyes. His pictures are very striking; the eyes have a kind, penetrating quality to them. He is perfectly free to do this.

But I have my own ideas.

The alkaline desert was here at the time these people were, this I have on the best scientific authority, even though the area surrounding the desert was swamp-like and no reasons can be given for the existence of a desert in this area at that time. It is obvious to me, then, that these people lived with some unusual arrangement in this desert; conditions were harsh in the extreme, and their food and water (not to mention linen, silver, and glass) had to come from somewhere else. I do not think it facetious at all to suggest, especially to anyone who has seen these caves, then, that in exchange for food, water, and other necessities these people were bound up in an unusual relationship with the desert. I have examined the caves closely enough myself to have determined that these were both a comfortable people, free from want, and a sedentary or perhaps even meditative people. This seems most reasonable.

I think it will be found too that the blue mounds with their white stone hearts have more to do with the desert than they have to do with the people alone. I think they might even be evidence of a bond between the people and the desert. I assume that the desert was the primary force in this relationship, but I could be wrong. It could have been the people who forged this relationship; we have no way of knowing exactly what they were capable of doing. Perhaps they were blue-skinned, and each had the thought of the desert at his heart, like the white stone in the blue earth, maybe this is the meaning. Perhaps this is what they are trying to say, that the desert is only a thought. I don't know.

There have been other suggestions, of course, mostly of a religious nature, but it is all conjecture. Many, of course, have avoided any mention of the blue mounds. In the years since I first discovered the caves I have noticed that they have been shifting a little to the north each year although the wall they are set in seems solid. I am apparently the only one to have noticed this. I have also been here recently when the caves were gone.

CONVERSATION

You are going to lose your shirt then.

No.

Let me ask you this: how are you going to get on out here? You told me you are sixty-one. You are very active, I can see that. Still, there is water to be carried every day, there is wood to be gathered, food — how long can you reasonably expect to live here with such limited resources? From where we sit I don't even see a juniper tree.

Have you ever seen a spider make a web? The thread comes out through little holes right above his ass. It is so thin you can hardly see it. He makes a trap for the bugs in the air. Before the web is made, before the bug is caught, the bug knows nothing of webs. It's as if the bug and the web didn't exist. The bug dies, he is eaten, he becomes material for a new web. The wind tears the old web down.

The point, then, is to hold still, to stay in one place?

Yes.

To wait. Is one supposed to wait for . . . what? Do you wait for something, for some *thing* to appear? Someone to come? Are you suggesting a mental thing?

You wait for yourself.

I'm already here.

No. Not really. You are stretched out like a string all over the place. The end of the string is here, the rest is there and there, back there in the mountains, on the other side. You must reel in the string, you must roll yourself up in a ball and then unravel yourself out here where you have the room and the clear light to study the condition of the threads.

Once you have the string all laid out, once you have repaired the worn pieces, you will establish certain points. Between these points you will line out the string until you have made a web, strong, very taut. The impact of a breeze at one edge will be felt at another. Sunlight will bounce when it hits, as though it were a trampoline. The sunlight will turn somersaults and you will know you have made the thing well. Then listen for the wind. The sound of the wind on the threads.

I must tell you this. I think this is bullshit.

It's bullshit because you are afraid your string will be too short. You are afraid it is too frayed, that you will be making knots all the time, that your web will be small and ridiculous.

I don't trust metaphors.

I am not talking metaphors. I am telling you the truth.

THE
SCHOOL

Look: from the size of the holes you can guess at the size of the bullets. These tiny ones, .22's. These, this cluster here, .30 - 30's maybe. Over here . . . this bunch in the floor. Eleven .44 magnums I think. Maybe a .45 automatic. Maybe whoever . . . maybe who made these holes in the floor was shooting *at* something, a rattlesnake. We have a lot of rattlesnakes. They come in here to get out of the sun.

All these holes scattered in the walls are from hunters. They come by looking for coyotes and rabbits and shoot at this because it's the only thing around. You'd never be able to tell what kind of bullets those holes are from, only if the shots came from inside or outside. That's a shotgun blast.

In the back here where the kitchen was . . . here . . . was this stove. Porcelain-faced, enameled handles, nickel-plated moulding. You can see what it was like. You can make out down here where someone's taken the name plate: see where the light affected the color of the metal over a period of years? Look at the way the oven door is caved in, like an old mouth. Shotgun did that. Four or five blasts with a shotgun. Look at this where they took the nickel-plated supports for the bread warmer, just hammered them off. Not even a wrench or a screwdriver. Well—maybe someone came by and scared them off.

This open space here is where the rear doors used to be, double doors of oak. I remember there were big brown knots in there, chocolate-colored and bigger than your fists. The brass plate where the latch slid across and the brass throw bolts for the second door both ran with the grain of the wood. (Don't step in that dog mess there.) They brought those doors over from the valley in 1921. Connie Whalen's father who owned the mines bought them.

These places were where the casement windows were. We'd open them in the hot weather and the front doors to get cross ventilation. There were fourteen panes of glass to each one. That was one of my jobs, to clean them. There's part of one of the window lattices out there in the rabbit brush.

This back room was for storage and where Miss Lamse kept some of her things. There was a day bed here and a little teak table over there that Miss Lamse brought back from San Francisco one summer. This plaster wall was put in after the building was built—you can see it's not as carefully done—look there where someone's pulled the plaster away how the lath has been set crooked. They did that when I was in the fourth grade on account of a fire regulation or something.

There was a door here of course. It had a steel handle that heated up in the afternoon because of the way the sun was on it coming through the windows. I can remember it that well. So much grease on these hinges they didn't make a sound; but the back doors squeaked. You know—here, look at this: even the window latches are gone. I knew they broke the glass and tore out the framing (you can see where they started a fire in the corner over there with some of the framing) but here somebody has gone to the trouble to take out the latches. Well, maybe they're worth something now. The windows were put in in 1922, the same year they put the building up. It all dates from 1922 except the plaster wall. (Look here at how hard this piece of hot dog is.)

I remember one morning Miss Lamse was having us clean up before we went home for Christmas. We were working on the desks (they used to be here, in rows, bolted to the floor); we were oiling the wood and the boys were scrubbing the floor—it was a hardwood floor, maybe maple, not this, this was the underfloor. Wait, here's a piece of the old floor. I don't know. Maybe it was maple. Well: we were oiling the desks and the boys were doing the floor to look nice for Christmas, and my best friend, Janet Ribbe, was doing the front windows, four to a side, when we heard Billy Wald screaming in the back room. Someone had hung up five dead rats on a string in the closet back there and spilled the guts out all over the floor. I think Tom Woodson did it but we never knew because Billy left school after that. He was smaller than the other boys, with anemia or something. I always worried about him. Janet Ribbe got sick to her stomach and went home. The boys cleaned it up and threw it all in the bushes. It was about two years later that Billy's father got drunk and shot him.

There were double doors here at the front too. Oak, like the others, and just as shiny, but the throw bolts and the handle were steel, not brass.

I remember the last time I was here when it was nice was when I graduated. Michael Peake and I were both graduated at the same time and went over to Cooley to the high school. That left nineteen here that year. The classes got smaller and smaller and about ten years later, oh, I don't know, maybe twelve, was the last class. By then the cinnabar was gone and the mine was shut down. Most of the people moved out to Cooley or over to Pilot Rock to work in the cement factory.

From then on the building was empty. Mr. Boeken, the county school superintendent, came and got the bell. He was going to give it to a school back east but I think he finally sold it to a museum. One night about seven years ago somebody threw a rope around the little cupola where the bell used to be and pulled it off with a pickup truck or something. By then people had been coming here for years, kids throwing rocks, out-of-state tourists. I don't know where the desks went. Or the books. Miss Lamse had about seventy-five books on a shelf at the back of the room that she left there when she died. There was a stove heater in the main room that's gone. I hope somebody used that maple from the floor. Mr. Whalen brought those boards two hundred miles on the train.

When the sun comes around this afternoon it will be an awful smell in here.

I come over sometimes and try and clean it out, burn up the garbage. I don't know what for. The last time I came over was about five years ago. The trouble with it, right from the beginning, was that it was too far away. The men put it up halfway between the town and the mines, thirty-one miles each way. They sank a well over there where that twisted thing is coming up out of the ground. But nothing ever grew up here, even when we planted. (Look there, down on the desert, at the size of that twister.) In this dry air it'll be a long time before it falls down. They'll have to push it over with a truck or something before they get rid of it.

THE
WIND

She is lying on her side in the dust; she is sighting along the curve of the desert floor. She is looking out underneath the round polished belly of an ant; the sun is pinging in the creases of his body as though he were made in sections of brown opaque glass. He is rolling a grain of white granite.

The granite cinder is half the size of the ant; it hangs at the lip of a crack. The ant pushes the boulder over the lip; she waits. She lays her ear tighter to the earth. She hears the boulder crashing to the bottom of the crack. She sees the ant slip into the crevice and disappear. She listens. She cannot hear him. She cannot hear him working his way down between the walls of the chasm. He is too careful.

She rolls over on her back. She closes her eyes and puts her hands out flat on her belly and pulls the warm dry air in through her nose and lets it puff out the sacks of her lungs until they are stiff against the inside of her ribs and there is a tingling across the top of her thighs. She imagines her hair slipping into the cracks beneath her, the long shiny black hair rolling like quicksilver off itself and over the alkaline dust and cascading down into the cracks, winding under the earth until her head is bound there like a rock pinned beneath a spider web. She feels a single drop of water bead on her forehead. It rolls over the bridge of her nose and across her cheek and evaporates.

She can feel the air bending like water around the soles of her feet and can feel it wash up her legs and pool in her belly, running back down through the dark hair and piling between her thighs; feel it moving in twirls up over her ribs, rushing up across her breasts, lying in the pocket of her throat, flowing up over her ears like hands burying in her hair; coming up the side of her leg, around below her hip under her back where there is space between her and the earth, back across her chest and gone, over her arm, tingle, finger, stretch, gone. Tongues of air roping like coils, water brushing dry leaving all the pores of her flesh puckered. With her head to one side she can see it touch out on the desert floor, gone.

She closes her eyes and lays her hands back on her belly.

The ant emerges from the crevice, his antenna filtering the air. He turns around and pulls a sage twig out of the crack. He sets off backwards and the spurs of the twig scratch the dust as he tugs. The noise alerts her; she turns to watch. The ant pulls the sage twig in jerks, levering against a boulder, twisting, until he has the twig at the edge of another crack. She rolls over on her side to place her ear tight against the white earth. He gives the twig a push and she hears it crash like a log batoning down the walls of a shale canyon tearing the earth loose. The ant slips into the crevice and she listens. She cannot hear him.

She rolls over on her stomach and lays her hands flat against the earth and shuts her eyes. She feels the prickling at the bottom of her spine as the moisture evaporates. The light covers her and she can feel its weight against the back of her legs; she can feel the thin blonde hairs on her arms absorbing it. A pressure against her ribs. Up over her back and the tiny hairs fold under the coming weight like rolling wheat sheening the light. It pools in the dimples of her flesh and washes out over her legs to her ankles and splashes over her heels and down over the soles of her feet and pushes against her toes. It moves through her hair pulling it up from her back and washing it over her shoulders, fluffing it flashing in the white light. It curves around to her face and she can feel it curve in the corner of her eye and run out over her nose vibrating the hairs on her cheeks. It tunnels up between her breasts and is gone.

She opens her eyes. She can feel the corner of her mouth wet against the earth. She folds her arms across her back and pushes her body against the weight. She rolls on her side and pulls her knees up. The sun blinks in the fold of her belly. The brown nipple of her white breast rests against a crack in the earth.

The ant is wrestling the husk of a seed. She watches him. He pulls the seed into the shade of a grey stone and leans against it. She can see the swirl of dust snaking over the desert floor toward them. It takes a long time, stopping and disappearing, then starting again, puffing the dust with sighs; the sun begins to fall before the swirl arrives. It comes suddenly over the grey stone like a wave breaking, bowls the seed from the ant's grasp into a foreign crevice and tumbles the ant away. Then it flattens out. It evaporates. It brushes her hips.

The girl rises to her knees and watches the sun

balance on the serrated ridge of the mountains. She puts on her clothes.

The ant emerges slowly from a cul-de-sac of dust. He walks across the desert. He disappears into the crevice after the seed.

The girl runs her fingers through her hair like combs and swings it free from her back. She puts on a jacket and twines her arms across her chest and feels the tingle on her thighs where the sun has lain. She fans her hands to a fire of small twigs. Her breath fogs. The puff of hair between her legs is kinked with warmth.

She is asleep. The ant emerges from the crack in the floor of the desert. He has the seed. The yellow light of the full moon glints on his round smooth belly.

COYOTE
AND
RATTLESNAKE

One time Coyote was out hunting and he met Rattlesnake. Rattlesnake was lying in the shadow of a rock at the edge of the desert.

"Coyote, where are you going?"

"I am hunting. I am looking for a fat rabbit. What are you doing?"

"I am waiting for mice."

Coyote sat down on a rock. He filled his mouth with air until his cheeks bulged, then let it leak out one corner of his mouth in a sort of whistling sigh.

"I'm getting tired of looking for food all the time, Rattlesnake. I spend too much time hunting. There are other things I would like to do."

"The winter is almost over. Spring is coming. There will be plenty of rabbits."

"Are you telling me you are doing well? I've seen you every day, waiting for mice. You catch nothing. Can't you see this is foolish?"

"It's the way things are."

"Oh I have no time for this sort of nonsense. I must be going."

Coyote only went off a little distance. He reached down and took a handful of pebbles and rolled them back and forth in his hand. He began flipping the pebbles casually at small targets, as though he were waiting for someone to come along or something to happen. He came back to where Rattlesnake was hidden.

"Rattlesnake, tell me, do you really mean to go

on like this year after year? Doing exactly as you are told?"

"How is that, Coyote?"

"Akasitah has said how we should live, that the coyote will hunt rabbits, that he will die at the hands of Shisa. He has said that the rattlesnake will live on the ground where he can see nothing and that he too will die at the hands of the Shisa. Who are the Shisa that I must hunt rabbits and step in traps as though I had no eyes? Who are the Shisa that you are beaten with sticks when they find you? We have all done as Akasitah said we should. But Akasitah is the friend of the Shisa. He is the enemy of all others."

"It is the other way around, Coyote."

"Rattlesnake, I have always believed you were the one who saw things best. When times were very bad you always made us see that in time things would be better. But you are wrong now. I have watched the Shisa. They are changing. They have become worse. I have watched you wait for mice. I have looked for rabbits. There are no rabbits. I am going to see Akasitah."

Coyote flung the few pebbles he had left onto the ground and left.

"I will see you when you come back," said Rattlesnake. He watched Coyote go. He watched for mice.

Akasitah lived in a white cloud at the top of a mountain that rose from the desert. The climb was long and very difficult. Coyote cut his feet on the rocks and cut the flesh of his hands. He fell exhausted on his face

when he reached the top. He did not move for a very
long time. When he opened his eyes he saw that the
top was flat and covered with grass. It was thicker than
any grass he had ever heard about. In the middle there
was a lake. The water was black. There was an otter
there.

You have come to see Akasitah about a new way
of life, said the otter. Coyote could hear him very well
even though he stood far away by the lake and was
looking off the other way. First you must purify
yourself, continued Otter.

"What shall I do," said Coyote, not knowing if he
could be heard.

You must build a small fire of twigs and sit there
by it through the night remembering all you can of
your life. In the morning when you see Akasitah at first
light you must say what it is you have to say quickly.
You cannot come back again another time and say it
again. If you are even a little afraid, Akasitah will go
away. You will spend the rest of your days looking
over your shoulder, running a little. If there is a trick in
your heart wrapped in pride, Akasitah will take away
the middle of all your thoughts. He will leave you only
with the ends. I tell you this, Coyote: if you do not
know why you are here, go home. In the morning it
will be too late.

Coyote did not know what to think. He wanted to
leave. Surely it was not this serious, only a little talking
with Akasitah. He thought of the long way up.
Rattlesnake would laugh at him. He would stay.

Coyote collected twigs and made the fire. The
night grew colder. There was no wind. Still it got
colder. The fire gave no heat and consumed no wood.

Coyote curled up to keep himself warm as best he could. And he thought. He thought of all he had seen of the Shisa. He had seen their cities from the mountains south of the desert. He could see beyond the curve of the earth from those mountains. He had watched the land change under the hand of Shisa. But this is not what bothered him. In the old days the Shisa had planted, they had put things back. Now they planted nothing, they returned nothing. Each winter there were fewer rabbits. Something could not come from nothing. Each day the Shisa came closer to the desert. It could not go on forever. They had changed it. They had broken the circle and made it straight like a stick.

Coyote watched the stars. He thought of the things in the desert. He thought of Rattlesnake waiting for the mice.

It was hard for Coyote to concentrate in the cold but he spent the night in thought. He remembered the day the Shisa had come loping over the shrub hills toward the desert. They came across a gully and it was full of rattlesnakes. They yelled and beat the snakes to death with sticks. Long after the snakes were dead they beat the snakes and threw them away, kicked them under the bushes. One of them, who was a little wiser, took this as a sign and led the rest of the Shisa away.

He remembered the time the Shisa had cracked open the sacred mountain with a great machine and taken the blue heart of the mountain away in chains. That is when he moved to the desert. He knew it would only be a short time after that before they came. The wise ones were dead. In a little while he would have to walk into the trap, as though he could not see.

That is what Akasitah had ordered. In the morning he would tell Akasitah it was no good.

Coyote watched the fire and listened to the stiff air resting on the tips of the thick grass until the sun rose and it lifted away.

When the first light came the fire burned itself out as though it were the sun setting. Coyote looked to the west for the last star in the black sky, to the north for Akasitah's white cloud, to the red mountains in the east, and to the south where he saw a sign of a good day in the yellow light.

Otter was standing far away by the edge of the lake. A wind came up and rippled the water. Coyote watched him but Otter did not move. Finally Otter said, Go a little to the north and wait.

Akasitah was there. Coyote could feel the warm spot in the wind. He began talking.

"Akasitah, I have come here to ask you to change your mind. Below it is chaos because of the Shisa. In a while there will be no place to go. I and all my friends, even the mountains, they will be taken away by the Shisa. It is said that you are wise and fair. How is it that the Shisa have come to this? Must I always be a coyote to the Shisa? Can I not be who I am? I ask you to change things. Let me walk out of the traps. Let Rattlesnake up off the ground so he can see something coming. Let these things happen or we will be no more. There will be nothing left. The Shisa will take even the desert."

There was a space in the wind.

Coyote, you see like a man with only one eye. The Shisa are like a great boulder that has broken away from the side of a mountain. The boulder makes a great noise as it comes down the side of the mountain. It tears away great chunks of earth and rock and breaks the trees like twigs, throwing up a cloud of dust against the sun and you are afraid for your life. There is no need to be afraid. It only seems this way because you have never known the world without the Shisa. You have spent your life under the boulder. I understand your fear.

Once there were no Shisa at all. When Stah-mi-atlosan sent me here I found the Shisa trapped inside the flowers before dawn. They asked to be set free and I put the sun in the sky and set them free. The rest you know. I tell you this, Coyote: they are like a boulder fallen off a mountain. Soon they will hit the earth at the bottom of the mountain and roll out into the desert leaving a little trail in the dust. The boulder will come to a stop. You can sleep on it at night. Do not worry. Go.

"Akasitah!" called Coyote. The warm spot in the wind was gone. Otter was gone. It was quiet. It took Coyote the rest of the day to get to the bottom of the mountain.

When he got to the desert he found Rattlesnake in the same place and even though it was the middle of the night he sat down and related everything that had happened and asked Rattlesnake his opinion.

"He told you everything there is to know," said Rattlesnake after a while.

"Still it is not clear to me."

"It is like this," said Rattlesnake. "The Shisa have become so large they are moving back into themselves. They have become like a storm turned inside out, that hurls lightning into itself until it is very small and then there is nothing.''

"How can you be sure of this?"

"You must watch, Coyote. You are always going off somewhere; that is why you understand nothing. When the storm comes across the hills toward the desert, watch how it turns itself into nothing. It goes over the desert like a small wind. These things are everywhere, Coyote, if you will open your eyes.''

Coyote stood up and walked off a little ways and stopped.

"Where are you going, Coyote?"

"I am going to hunt for rabbits."

Coyote went off to the highest hill he could find and sat down with his back against a rock. He scanned the horizon for a cloud and when he found one he settled down to wait.

He wondered if Rattlesnake had ever lied.

DIRECTIONS

I would like to tell you how to get there so that you may see all this for yourself. But first a warning: you may already have come across a set of detailed instructions, a map with every bush and stone clearly marked, the meandering courses of dry rivers and other geographical features noted, with dotted lines put down to represent the very faintest of trails. Perhaps there were also warnings printed in tiny red letters along the margins, about the lack of water, the strength of the wind and the swiftness of the rattlesnakes. Your confidence in these finely etched maps is understandable, for at first glance they seem excellent, the best a man is capable of; but your confidence is misplaced. Throw them out. They are the wrong sort of map. They are too thin. They are not the sort of map that can be followed by a man who knows what he is doing. The coyote, even the crow, would regard them with suspicion.

There is, I should warn you, doubt too about the directions I will give you here, but they are the very best that can be had. They will not be easy to follow. Where it says left you must go right sometimes. Read south for north sometimes. It depends a little on where you are coming from, but not entirely. I am saying you will have doubts. If you do the best you can you will have no trouble.

(When you get there you may wish to make up a map for yourself for future reference. It is the only map you will ever trust. It may consist of only a few lines

75

hastily drawn. You will not have to hide it in your desk, taped to the back of a drawer. That is pointless. But don't leave it out to be seen, thinking no one will know what it is. It will be taken for scribble and thrown in the wastebasket or be carefully folded and idly shredded by a friend one night during a conversation. You might want to write only a set of numbers down in one corner of a piece of paper and underline them. When you try to find a place for it—a place not too obvious, not too well hidden so as to arouse suspicion—you will begin to understand the futility of drawing maps. It is best in this case to get along without one, although you will find your map, once drawn, as difficult to discard as an unfinished poem.)

First go north to Tate. Go in the fall. Wait in the bus station for an old man with short white hair wearing a blue shirt and khaki trousers to come in on a Trailways bus from Lanner. You cannot miss him. He will be the only one on the bus.

Take him aside and ask him if he came in from Molnar. Let there be a serious tone to your words, as if you sensed disaster down the road in Molnar. He will regard you without saying a word for a long time. Then he will laugh a little and tell you that he boarded the bus at Galen, two towns above Molnar.

His name is Leon. Take him to coffee. Tell him you are a journalist, working for a small paper in North Dakota, that you are looking for a famous desert that lies somewhere west of Tate, a place where nothing has ever happened. Tell him you wish to see the place for yourself.

If he believes you he will smile and nod and sketch a map for you on a white paper napkin. Be careful. The napkin will tear under the pressure of his blunt pencil and the lines he draws may end up meaning nothing at all. It is his words you should pay attention to. He will seem very sure of himself and you will feel a great trust go between you. You may never again hear a map so well spoken. There will be a clarity in his description such that it will seem he is laying slivers of clear glass on black velvet in the afternoon sun. Still, you will have difficulty remembering, especially the specific length of various shadows cast at different times of the day. Listen as you have never listened before. It will be the very best he can do under the circumstances.

Perhaps you are a step ahead of me. Then I should tell you this: a tape recorder will be of no use. He will suspect it and not talk, tell you he must make connections with another bus and leave. Or he will give you directions that will bring you to your death. Make notes if you wish. Then take the napkin and thank him and go.

You will need three or four days to follow it out. The last part will be on foot. Prepare for this. Prepare for the impact of nothing. Get on a regimen of tea and biscuits and dried fruit. On the third or fourth day, when you are ready to quit, you will know you are on your way. When your throat is so thick with dust that you cannot breathe you will be almost halfway there. When the soles of your feet go numb with the burning and you cannot walk you will know that you have made no wrong turns. When you can no longer laugh at all it is only a little further. Push on.

It will not be as easy as it sounds. When you have walked miles to the head of a box canyon and find yourself with no climbing rope, no pitons, no one to belay you, you are going to have to improvise. When the dust chews a hole in your canteen and sucks it dry without a sound you will have to sit down and study the land for a place to dig for water. When you wake in the morning and find that a rattlesnake has curled up on your chest to take advantage of your warmth you will have to move quickly or wait out the sun's heat.

You will always know this: others have made it. The man who gave you the map has been here. He now lives in a pleasant town of only ten thousand. There are no large buildings and the streets are lined with maples and a flush of bright flowers in the spring. There is a good hardware store. There are a number of vegetable gardens—pole beans and crisp celery, carrots, strawberries, watercress and parsley and sweet corn—growing in backyards. The weather is mixed and excellent. Leon has many friends and he lives well and enjoys himself. He rides Trailways buses late at night, when he is assured of a seat. He can make a very good map with only a napkin and a broken pencil. He knows how to avoid what is unnecessary.